CSU Poetry Series XXVII

Another Body

poems by Stephen Tapscott

*for Anne
in friendship
Steve
Tapscott*

Cleveland State University Poetry Center

Acknowledgments

My thanks to the editors of the periodicals that published earlier versions of some of these poems:

AGNI REVIEW: "You"

ANTAEUS: "Narcissus"

AMERICAN POETRY REVIEW: "In Fairfield, Connecticut," "Letter to an Immigrant" (section #29)

CAROLINA QUARTERLY: "Gallinules"

EPOCH: "Island," "*Laude*," "Leaving Plainfield"

HUMANITAS: (Univ. of Notre Dame; 1988 memorial issue for Joseph M. Duffy): "The Ring"

LITERARY REVIEW: "This"

MISSOURI REVIEW: "Because she is pregnant," "In the darkness of the body," "When the water broke"

NEW ENGLAND REVIEW/BREAD LOAF QUARTERLY: "I Write"

PARIS REVIEW: "Oats"

PEMBROKE: "Comrade"

PEQUOD: "Letter to an Immigrant" (sections #1-9)

PLOUGHSHARES: "Appaloosa," "Chronic," "*El Zoologico*," "Hank," "Landscape with Mares and Foals"

TENDRIL: "Forger of Vermeer"

"*A travelling scroll*," first appeared in the AWP NEWSLETTER, 1983. "In light" was the cover-poem of the 1985 catalogue from Louisa Solano's Grolier Book Shop in Cambridge, Massachusetts.

I offer this book to those who have shaped it: to Sophia Black, Steven Cramer and Hilary Rao, David Kridler, Stephen Massey, Andrew Rosing, and Susan Tarrant.

Several of these poems are dedicated to individuals:
"The Ring" is for Joseph M. Duffy, Jr. (1924-1988)
"Comrade" is for A. R. Ammons
"The Island" is for Roman Jakobson and Krystyna Pomorska, and
"Letter to an Immigrant" is for Andrei Ruzhnikov and Sue Ruzhinkov.

For their generous support while these poems were in progress, I would like also to thank the Karolyi Foundation (Vence, France), the MacDowell Colony, and the Artists Foundation (with funds from the Massachusetts Council on the Arts and Humanities).

Funded Through
Ohio Arts Council

727 East Main Street
Columbus; Ohio 43205-1796
(614) 466-2613

Contents

I

One of the evidences of the immortality of the soul, it has always seemed to me, is the awful solitude in which a soul here lives.

—R. W. Emerson, *Journal*

The Ring

Sometimes at night I wake up.
Lying alone in the dark,
    a grown man without children,
I listen to what is there,
    though I know nothing is there,
nobody else in the house.
    Like others I am used to
sleeping alone; like others
    I know that certain silence
solitude in a quiet room
    engenders—thin, like a ringing,
like the jingling silver coins
    of a foreign city where you
find yourself visiting—. This is
    different. It is not fear, not
human, or particular.
    It is not of *me*, at all:
like overhearing something
    I'd somehow always known,
as if something in the huge
    air, or else the air itself,
were turning, and I felt it,
    and I were turning with it,
knowing. And somehow that—how
    can I say it?—that *motion*
had come to listen, as if
    it woke me up to attend
to me: almost tenderly,
    almost purposefully, as if,
lacking a body, it
    needed me, in the fullness
of its work. I do not know
    that it even has a will
or a name, or appetite,
    only that it moves and asks:
but I would like to draw myself
    in a circle around it,
as if to hold it in me,

as if—if I could lie still
enough, smooth as a breath, it
    might find, briefly, what it needs:
as a child might hold a coin
    to a page and crayon a
firm black line around it
    to serve as the sun. The light
swells, in its black and yellow
    stripes, from its quarter in the
upper corner; radiant
    it turns across the square world
of the picture: on the tall
    flat paddles of trees, across
the house's circumflex roof,
    without harm, hardly touching
them it pours through the children
    standing outdoors one by one,
aligned with one another
    by height, in the order of
authority among them.
    The sky is empty-wide; they
bend their arms out slightly from
    their bodies: elbows, orange hands
and huge fingers, heads round as dimes,
    with eyes, mouths, brown spikes of hair.
Light fills even the hollow
    bodies of the animals—
instincts the size of the children,
    smiling and baring their teeth.
Strong in the satisfactions
    of its outline, the light informs
all the represented world:
    even the red and upright
rootless tulips, the green slab
    of grass. Diagonal black,
yellow, black, yellow, black: how
    precisely the light rolls! like
a parental power. Like
    the spokes of a great high wheel.

Hank

Because he sometimes bored himself with thinking
my father taught himself things. Or because
he was an American man: back from Saipan,
married early, stuck in a stupid job
for the kids, and farm-chores after that.
Or it may have been a kind of silent booze,
he was so silent: sitting in the chair
in his room, which we were not to enter,
in the tobacco penumbra that smelled of hickory
and circled him slowly, marbelling the light

of the upright lamp beside him, he read
for years. I remember *The History of Flight*,
the *Imitatione Christi*, the photographs
of Chinese bronzes Mother wrapped
for Christmas, that went into his room
and kept him there, evenings, for a week. Then
for a while it was the law: *constructs*, he said,
and distinctions. Then anatomy—:
Stubbs on horses first, the stronger fact,
then Gray on human bodies. I turned

my eyes off when he tried to show me, once.
Which was why, I guess, he kept a skeleton
on a hook-stand near him, dried and wired whole.
Mamma refused to dust it; no one said
exactly how he got it, when, or from whom.
I knew only that it smiled above
behind him, that he told me it was nothing
to fear, that he called it his friend "Hank."
I stood by his chair and looked up, then.
And how I came to be

there I do not remember, in the daytime
when my father was at work, and across
the pale oak floor the varnished light
made the room feel hollow. I was just there,

and a little lonely. I watched it—I mean, *him*—
because the face was turned away
and he could not see me. As I looked up
from the thighbones I could see the light
pass through the ribs, the dark bars shaped
by open space, like the keys on our piano.

If I wanted, then, to lift his hand
and set it on my shoulder, and feel
the white quiet weight of the truth
touch me once, through my tee-shirt . . . well, I held
back, being a boy. He looked away, Hank.
How he knew it was a man I never
did understand, the friend in my father's secret
study; though I supposed there were ways
to decipher such puzzling things. Even then.
Even so long dead and clean of the flesh.

Appaloosa

In spring, when the earth turns
to food, and the mares thicken
with what they have kept hidden
through winter in their bodies,

and between her legs weeks early
the sac grew
of the thin bluish milk that is the first need,
in the last days

she'd come reluctantly, if at all,
to the wooden barn, preferring
the other heavy mares for company:
and when the time came withdrawing

even from them somewhere
she knew, to the hardwood valley
of the pasture, the bay of the slag fence, wherever
she had chosen

to do what must be done.
And did it, alone,
working her mute body.
I understand little of this,

except that once
I was young,
that it did not seem mysterious
but love, an ordinary duty, to follow her

track through the mud and the milkweed
path down, chest-high, to the stream-bed sump-land
where I could hear her,
bleeding. A night had passed,

and the ripping,
and the crying out: now she stood
bending to him, the pure form,
licking the film from his eyes, a little

fearful. He curled across the wide vervain,
an Appaloosa colt—
though the mare was chestnut, the sire high bay.
Such things happened,

Appaloosa:
how an ordinary pair
makes a strange one, born strong but
roan through the chest, clear-starred but

stippled white through the haunch, and
striped hooves, and blue eyes.
Those days
farmers drowned them, made mares refuse them;

hell-to-break, pepper-minded, wicked clever—
impossible to predict, or to breed.
Or if they do, two of a kind,
the colt is normal

but trouble. Broken, they run like fire.
I watched him almost-sleep, the first I'd seen.
She muzzled Necco wafers from my pocket;
we watched him breathe. He watched us watch.

Three days, my father
took the animal. So I never learned
what happened to him
that he was strange,

and marked fire in an older world,
and unprofitable.
My father never told me, and I never asked,
and I was afraid.

Comrade

Now it has turned hot. Sometimes
    it's phenomenal, the heat, at night,
pulling heart-water from things,
    from the pastel grass, rising to hot mists
at dawn, burning them off by noon.
    Tonight I woke up
across a white sheet, in a fish-glaze
    of sweat the night had

pulled from my body as I slept,
    and walked out from this underground apartment
through the window to the darkened lawn.
    Here it is empty,
a little wind, the moist
    across my chest cracks and slips a little,
and my skin feels tight,
    cooler and truer.

So it does not seem surprising
    that the toad,
in his snotty overcoat,
    fumbles his way across the open lawn calling
here I am   here I am
    or that he gorps
and splays at my feet, working
    the thick reptilian bubble of his throat,

chewing the new air   *here I am,*
    Comrade: as if, being so precisely
toad he belongs
    precisely where he flops.
It is much too late—too dark—to see
    his fingers, which I imagine
veiny as bean-sprouts, spatulate and coiled around
    something of value to him: some sweet

plump grub he has caught, something
        one must look for
needily to find. And that his belly
        would be pale, a little pouch of knuckles
he rolls on,
        falling into place.
What is this tenderness?
        as if I remembered it:

I was on an island. The wind across
        the dunes was hot, and the almost-vertical light
glanced across the water,
        which was soft-green
and cooler, even, than it looked,
        seductive. Shifting from foot
to foot on the scalded sand
        I watched the lifeguard

churn ashore and drag it
        to the higher harder ground.
It had longish fingers,
        perfectly white, hairless and
curled under into the wrists, and yet it was
        somehow almost a public thing:
every which way they turned it,
        it acquiesced.

It must have been in the water
        a long time already, because it moved
fluent as the water. A tablespoon of salt
        foamed at each nostril,
and the eyes,
        which would have been brown
except for the little lens of gelatine that filmed them,
        did not shift to watch

as the men rolled the bundle
    in a blanket and emptied it,
jabbing hiccoughs of fluid from the blue
    puffy belly. We knew it was
much too late already, but we worked there
    a long time anyway,
the pale bathers helping
    or standing by in a ring, loyal and helpless

(helping by standing by), while the huge guard
    pumped at the chest, kneading
rhythm—breath—
    through the violet mouth,
kissing the dead man till the truth
    we were fighting with was stronger,
then stronger again—:
    till it was irresistible.

In Fairfield, Connecticut

I was angry with the earth,
which wanted my uncle
so ruthlessly,
dismantling muscle

by muscle,
all that spring,
while the dogwood
displayed across the window

and he watched it happen,
lifting the broken symmetrical pinks
and whites, in attitudes of hands
above the ground. Man

to man I attended
his body with sponges,
till an old shame
plucked at us both

and he chose dignity,
turning to look way, and took
to wearing his flat tweed cap,
fresh from County Kerry in 1919,

weeks of afternoon
on the rented bed
and pulled at the glass straw
and leaned

against my shoulder
propped toward the light
and worked at breath, giving me
what a woman must know,

a live strange creature
pressing itself, becoming
its needy weight, against the body,
and that perfect rage.

The Squirrel

has found the thistle-seed I spread
    up the steps to lure him near
the feeder at the window. March's dead
    and chronic snow has numbed his fear

to foolishness—or honed it, maybe,
    into will. I recognize
this one: the summer-baby,
    all brass and fluff, who terrorized

the chickadees, so young
    he commandeered the feeder,
sweeping his tail, squandering bread-crumbs
    to the wind. Need has made him neater

now. He cups the separate grains, black
    as syllables, fine as pins
in his paws. He takes
    his time: turning, considering

each, kissing at each, till it goes
    soft, and he can chew.
He eats completely, sniffs the snow
    to see if he has missed a clue—

after so much winter, food is style, is luck;
    best not to waste. So pad by pad
he inches the length of my porch
    up the track he prints

on the ice-crust till he arrives
    in confidence: upright
on his bowed tail, cuffing his whiskers,
    proud of himself, to trust

his intuition, and his nose, and the small
    essential signs I sprinkled
for him to find, the line
    he works to the still, the blind,

the feeder, his image in the steely
    window, and behind it, me. . .

Is this what human parents feel?

    How lonely God must be!

Leaving Plainfield,

I left my friends, and turned left down the hill
on Highway 2 and got as far as Plattsburgh
and the bridge, the silver nudge of Lake Champlain,
before it did not hurt to think of them.
Along the valley single painted cottages
huddled under pines, their cordwood stacked
and mounded in bindweed. It was August,
and the evidence of August
gathered over the meadow and the open lake.
I tried to count
the random sailboats rounding the island
but the numbers revolted, insisting
one white boat and *one white boat* and *one* and *one.*. . .

    Homer knew it,
    listing the names of the lost Greeks
    as if the name were not a cloud, desire,
    but a second body.

The great lovers knew it
and were alone, pushing their names against
the form of the other, half afraid
that wild inhuman heat would meld them
and make them stay
together, brutally familiar, like animals
or antique gods. We have learned instead
to lie with our bodies, believing what we do not say
except in touch cannot be reduced. . . . Difficult even
to think so, holding the lonely bodies
of my friends in memory, raging
consolations, inflecting the verbs of us
tacitly, our lives
we do not tell each other much
any more, our care is that tacit.

That is why Patroclus is the hero of the *Iliad*,
strapping on his friend's armor,
knowing he would die twice,
body and name, carrying his friend's other life.
   Because
if love is the merger of two solitudes,
what shall we call this?:
the lover who becomes the other's armor,
the friend of his name, as marriage
can not? The strange part is,
Achilles let him go.
They never even heard of Homer.

Remembering him, I no longer wonder
how a man walks—through a field
of wild carrot, say, in August—and feels
suddenly he is walking
over a glass window. All that he sees is there,
and also what he knows, is there. Because

   love is the bravest double-talk,
   a love that is friendship
   first. Because locked in a name
   self, or anonymous together, unloosed,
   we are doubly lonely.

Beyond the Inlet Road, one white boat
leans past the far island,
articulated by fog. My friends: because
despite the affection, and thick August gathering
in the throat of the hills, and despite the fields
of wild carrot across the field
of fossils, despite the consolations
that do ripen, mostly, the longer we know
one another, this one raw life is not enough.
That is why we are lonely,
each life half

of a perfect metaphor. And why
we fall, each of us,
reluctantly into words—because
that is the closest our bodies can come
to something unreachably simple:
as, waking at night, a man and a woman
will find themselves suddenly
shy and half-ashamed, needing to explain,
in the bed where they have slept for years.

Because she is pregnant and
full of her California

girlhood, thirty years'
longing and forgiveness, these weeks
Rebecca has filled the house with poppies.
They are so pure,
California-gold-fleshed and their lines
unblurred, I would like to hold her
for a moment, for what she brings to them—

though she is my friend's new wife, and we are shy.
She has set them in a jelly-jar in the thin kitchen light,
where they pull toward the window and remember
to turn open, turn closed, according to their first rhythm.
This morning she warms her fingers around the teacup,
she rubs her narrow shoulders, she is tired;
the baby rolled and fumbled through her sleep.

And I wonder she can watch them so long
so intently:
as if they were simple poppies, and watching them were
also simple, according to a first rhythm
we thought we had forgotten and had not.
Loss is not the mystery.
The body, which remembers and continues: that is
        the mystery.

Oats

I stood by the dark barn and called
and called to her by name,
into the labyrinth of stalls
and webs and smells, where I could see
nothing in the bent light. And when she came
she came bowing to me

out of the darkness,
bending her neck through the half-gate
to test my purposes:
winter-rugged, high-eared, calm
and skeptical of gifts. Her breath
spread its fur across my palm

as I offered it, the ball of her nose
worked nimbly as fingers: she picked
at the oats I held out
scrupulously,
as though they might be attached
to my skin in some secret human way

she couldn't see. When they were gone,
as evenly as she'd come
she turned
and walked off into the barn
and left me watching. So I never learned
more than she'd offered:

whether she were sheltering
a coldwater foal, putting herself
between me and the breathing
fact, unused to the December air
and the strange hands and the mansmell
I carried; or whether an old fear

pulled her away; or whether the barn
was simply empty
and out of the wind, familiar
as I wasn't, when the oats were finished.
It wasn't nostalgia, nor mystery,
nor simple creature-pity after loss

I stood with
when she turned,
bending like a great fish,
and leaned back into the dark.
But it was distant and familiar:
the oatchaff sprinkled its sting

across my fingers and I recognized,
advancing, what I hadn't guessed:
that we had come to this. Here. This.

II

The Island

Either the tangled water surrounds this island
or this island rises over water like a man
awakening. We do not know. Mostly we do not mind
not knowing. We are guests. Voluptuous palms
dim the inland as we dock; water repeats
under us the sky in waterlight;

we walk the gangway dizzied, hanging under light
and over light. Then grit and root: the island
hardens. A moment; our bodies repeat
the deck-roll of the boat, someone staggers, the man
who ferried us casts off, waving, his palm
receding in the glare like a mind

withdrawing, down a line of the mind's
habitual work. The wake smoothes; we watch the light
go green, stiffen, down the totem-line of palms
to a house on the headlands of the island.
The chauffeur, a genial obscure man,
vanishes. . . . That was the first day. To repeat

the story later was a consolation, repeat
the few clean facts the mind
assembles into legend. No one knew the man
or woman whose guests we were, or dream. Daylight
widened us. We roamed the house. We mapped the island,
sniffing the wind. Some learned the shell and palm

and sea-bird codes. We harvested, cooked on palm-
wood fires. One climbed the roof and would repeat,
shouting, the lack of news. Our legends filled: *the island
comprises. . . . the island contains. . . .* We did not mind
we always almost knew for certain, never quite. The light
included us. And there were others: intenser than a man,

thick, bristled, suffering slower than a frightened man
or ordinary animals, they watched from the strong palm
shadows. Flexed their snouts, waited. Moved to us, oddly
    light
approaches, on split feet. Grunt, pause. Repeat
the utterance: as if, large with pity, an articulating mind
stuttered, stranded in a body as on an island.

Were we their guests, then, on their island? —as if a human
will could grow so pure of mind. *We knew; we chose.* The
    palms
repeat like flesh, like flesh. *We trot; we snort; we root in
    light.*

Laude

He was a face
photographs improved:
gaunt, Phidian, scrupulously shaved.
Old pictures gave him a foreign body,
grinning in the mineral light
of Athens, or the islands, his arm linked
loose around some friend his age.

Teaching at home, he loved
the particular histories of things:
etymologies that reached toward verbs,
a recipe for avgolemono soup,
the mahogany clock that made the hour
sound large, in his white apartment.
He sat with his back to the window.

Autumn and spring he led me
through the *Iliad*, clause by clause
to the death of Hector. Spent a week
on the last great feast. Began the *Philoctetes*
and never finished. Just once, before commencement,
we digressed, laying aside the copy
of Sophocles we shared—and worked instead

on the Sappho papyrus discovered by accident,
in strip-papers winding a Coptic mummy.
Eighteen years old, half in love
with love-and-death, I churned
through the harsh dactyls and the unfamiliar verbs
of longing: till he lifted the book from my lap
and read the poem

through in a low voice.
What did I know? It was late
in the afternoon; over his shoulder
the rain had ended, Commonwealth Avenue
gave up a grey light, and men wrapped
in bright metallic cars, shining toward destinations,
flew to the right and the left of him terribly fast.

You

as if I had imagined you
while your body in shadow on the flowered shower-curtain
     caresses itself

and I in cooling flesh and hardening a little
in goosebumps breathing the warm half-body
steam of the bath, shaving, the sunlight

tilts across the ceramic wall and fills
the mirror from behind, in broken and exact
colors of the spectrum: what makes them
seem so familiar, so like propositions? so naked

and a little bored, alert-as-if-asleep, I construct on the wall
     thinking
a square on the diagonal of one tile square and wonder
how it reproduces, the square of the hypotenuse
the sum of the squares on the other two sides—Pythagoras,
     I think,
though I do not remember ever actually having learned that
     theorem—,

and shiver in my damp towel and surprised flesh
     remembering
what I seem never to have learned:
I do not remember ever not having known you,
having known you
somehow in memory, you
in your body, only more exactly:

must be I must always
have known it, contained you, in the soul, so that
knowing, now, feels like remembering
what I never learned: so that the soul,
remembering with knowing what it knew without learning,
must be forever, must always have been—must will be—,

dearest, because of you: with you and in you, your body
     there, I remember
nights of love with you so married they are almost
     indistinguishable—
you were innumerable women, summarized, and I desiring
     you
desired them and found you and held you in purified
     remembering:
though I'm not sure now you could hear anything I'd try to
     tell you,
while your shadow on the flowered curtain rinses itself
     thinner—still, here, now—
you I imagined also out of desire, out of my need for you, in
     your only body.

Chronic

If time is our sickness, friend, health in the flesh
would be a rare visit. I could believe it.
Today when you called at five in the morning to say
Delta flight seven. . . . *depart.* . . . *arrive.* . . . *depart.* . . .

I was already dreaming your voice; what I needed was
your information. When you arrive
it will be as if you had already been here, and gone,
and come back. Remember

the sticks of forsythia we broke
from the naked hedge to mark the border garden?
Now, nearing Easter—I can show you—they bubble
a white froth from their pores, rooting, already many

urgent little trees. It will be cool
April here, and older light. The maples have begun
where they left off in autumn, red
at the reaching tips and swollen in the keys.

All winter they stood, the mature trees,
as if they were beyond desire.
I wonder does it hurt them, to be pulled
out of themselves? They do not say so.

In this they do not resemble us, who mostly suffer
our changes together. Maybe in the end
we will remember each other simply, as a good idea
the flesh took for a time.

Nantucket: The Stranding

It would not be denied, the huge
thing, nudging
its otherworldy body up the beach
through the shallows

into air,
flying its expert fins, to blow
draft after draft while the curious human
crowd circled

and hushed:
               till the authorities came
with grapples and winched it
back to its place, in the deeper water.

*

It returned, it would
deny itself, the right-whale
pushing its absolute body
over sand, spraying

prisms and its weird call
among us. It seemed to be
thinking: the side-eye lolled
in the dominant head, mostly body

and already melting in
scarves of oil, uttering
its high inhuman cry, spouting
half salt air, half water.

*

The third day it was back,
the dumb fish,
gorping and throwing its notched flukes
and starting to stink.

Who knew
what it wanted? Or what
would satisfy it but this denial
and display? On the forehead

reasonable gulls
drilled at barnacles. It lay
as if it could not forgive itself,
humped and spasming in the public sand.

Gallinules

Oddly, I console myself
that you are gone:
saying much remains,
much deserving

of wonder. Even the black ducks
have returned, those
that pleased you so,
in intricate raw March.

They have survived themselves,
and the vivid insistence
of breeding, and summer
in the riceland marshes.

Sad materialists, they gather
on the ridges of the supple water.
They do not notice, where they bobble
in the late light, how each

pulls behind him a red
abandonment of water,
dissolving. How lightly they work
across the great depth!

Pushing and
pushing the wild ducks swim,
and the slash behind them heals,
water into water into water.

This

This is the sadness
the angels knew, watching you
sleep, your face
clarified, the child of you

rising as through cleared water.
We have never been younger than this,
not as children, not as first lovers
surprised to be flesh.

This is the sorrow the angels accepted
bending to the lighted cave
and the child, whose body
enclosed in itself

stopped all other imaginings.
Unfolding their musical wings, poised
in that huge air, the angels knew
all things had been possible.

A travelling scroll,

brown rice-ink on silk.
On the long fabric
by Chou-an of the late Kung
Dynasty, "Reign
of Difficult Freedoms,"
I see the landscape,
a man descending
a mountain, which
broadens as it unrolls.
In the folds of his
cloak he carries something
I cannot see, and
past him the sky rains
stipples in the west.
The man crosses the
mountainside, in one
high bend of the road,
forever. Ahead
the landscape where he
would travel, homeward,
thickens. He is small
in the vertical air
and the road opaque
and specific and
quiet as willows,
and the echo-bridge
arched on the ravine
the man approaches
from the upper left:
it, too, is silent,
lifting. Below it,
fish of vague colors
glide farther downstream
diagonally,
to guide the eye down
the spiral structure
of the hill, and leap

sometimes into air,
        piercing the water,
pass under the small
        wooden house on stilts,
fine in perspective,
        in the right corner.
Through vistas between
        the man and his home,
orchards, moraines, bent
        pines cling to a slope,
a farm-boy herding
        cattle on a path
that curls. You can hear,
        almost, what they say
as they pass, the high
        ritual greeting of men
whose work is to watch
        and who meet other
men only seldom:
        it sounds like the man
who made it, his hand
        descending from the
high important place
        he suggested with
empty white, moving
        down to work the earth.
Think of him watching
        as he had, perhaps,
for years, through the nights,
        while his wife slept
alone in her room:
        as he coaxed the ink
around the heifer and
        asked her to shift those
bony polls a little
        and to look sideways,
grumpy through her horns—
        yes! like that!—at the
herd-boy with his sharp

greenhazel switch: did
he laugh to himself
in his night-room? (what
can art share? with whom?)
I see the landscape
is within the self:
because it is hard
to explain, it can
be shown, in distance,
and travelled. It can
not be known, wholly.
Faith is the structure:
a form constructed
to descend, its clear
information lines
drawn longingly, down,
in, toward a house: look:
through the paper walls,
the form of someone
choosing to stand there,
as if the cottage
were made to seem this
clearly to surround
that embodiment
and the brazier,
its frail stalk of smoke
rising, rising: past
long mountains that lift,
losing themselves in
white, blending to a
sky the color of
trout—and of longing—
watchfulness—and failed
prayer, ordinary
familiar failure—

On the Corridor

The gods have answered my prayers.
You have grown older
in the face and body.
I thought it would be harder

to forgive that image
that resembled you. But
meeting like this, on an empty corridor,
I find it nothing to remember

that self: who wore black
because I enjoyed you in black,
and who desired me. Now you have taken
to pastels, which flatter, and to looser lines.

The gods permitting, I find now I can wish for you
what you always wanted: one after another,
night after pale night, may you attract
the lovers you deserve.

Under the Boardwalk

"It almost doesn't matter who you are.
. . . . or would you prefer warm lies? *Your body's*
love is an idea I remember

of you before I knew you; gold-summer
promises; moon-shine on the mirror-lake: etc.
It almost doesn't matter who you are,

you're here. I want to fuck you; you desire
me, or I'll do. That's what the sad flesh's
love is: an idea. I remember

how the wiser gods used to appear on earth,
animals heads founded on human bodies.
It almost doesn't matter who you are

or want. You could imagine another
man and call it me. Fine: it works both ways,
Love. Is an idea I remember

less true than you? Your eyes reflect me. We're
alone. So close them; relax; undo these;
it almost doesn't matter who you are;
love is an idea I remember."

Forger of Vermeer

This blue, my represented angel

lifting her trumpet, might be
the authentic blue
of Delft sky surrounding irises,
or the intermediate
blue of beached waves as they drop their shapes,
or even nearly the mind's carnal blue, blue as the robe
of an angel, appearing.

It is not his blue.

For him the factual cloth
crumples on the model's shoulder:
as if—for him—the angel were
indistingishably the model,
or such a wild longing
as realizes *angel*—
not giving her a face, but finding hers.

In the deep room she turns her head.

In the ordinary light
her only body
informs the blue linen.
How surely she stands there
possible at the window! Surely
I have been wrong, believing one solitude
approaches another.

That chord of light along her hand

is not an instrument
but an accomplished solitude.
It touches the world's body.
It turns in the eye.
Indistinguishable
that cryptic need,
that public angel.

III

Letter to an Immigrant

It is a long way to God.
                    —Russian proverb

God bless the Czar
and keep him far
away from us.
                    —Yiddish/Russian proverb

Andrei Yevgenievich,
                I am here
to send you some welcome
to America, and what I have
to tell you fills the window:

this arc of pale Massachusetts sky,
the sand-bitten soil of my place,
a scattering of apple-trees—:
not these, exactly, but what gathers them,

the mapped longing
of a single self, one
of many Americas,
composed.

And past the several barns, that one
lean squirrel (*byelka*: they are grey here)
in the wooden orchard,
figuring a new nest before winter.

It's almost ready,
the scrappy abstract loft he's worked
of birch wattle, flim, heaped leaves.
We will see if it will hold him.

*

In the old maps, with Europe at the center,
America is that white
destination, pure
latitude, where public monsters

thrash the meticulate little ships
that are so brave,
sailing out singly toward the empty
selvedge. Here where the whales lolled

over acres of paper
hugely innocent
Andrei we are:
at large here quietly

in Pontiacs and Plymouths,
while the far hills drop off
like waves along the broken
white center line.

*

You should know America
was not so much discovered
as invented, drafted

novelty on surmise
on novelty: an earnest, unsendable letter.
In America, Andrei, you may move

often: soon
it will even seem natural, the highway
gathering to a green point,

folding the map that folds
back on itself,
our palimpsest.

You'll learn to hear the Indian,
the steady loamy vowelling,
in the names that survive,

and in those that follow, superimposed,
a history of the future: Providence.
Philadelphia. Corpus Christi. Los Angeles.

*

In this America, space
builds toward time,
concretely: we say Washington lies
nine hours from Boston,

California *six days* from here.
Most everyone you meet will have a sibling
in the West, parents who have gone south
to retire, to invest

in real-estate, to die
tanned. A family means
a web of timing:
we seldom correspond.

Therefore an American
is a spider,
as modest Whitman says:
noiseless, patient.

What bouys him is
space, wide
intersections, the random ringing
shiver of news through the wires.

*

In America, Andrei, one afternoon
at the bell: a warm anonymous
woman, her smile a harness.
How welcome she will seem
to a man who works at home! Bending
her slender shoulders through the frame
she will step in—
you will assemble,

as is your right. Your ease and hope
confound you: you have come
so far for this! She will explain:
that she is a Witness, a specie of Prophet,
some kind of Saint. Has come to offer you a program
of salvation. Will you accept her
illustrated literature
with no obligation? You pose some neutral, some

half-personal question; she smiles and obliges—:
comes from Zion, or Navoo, or
Salt Lake. Yes, does enjoy her
missionary pilgrimage. Meets such
interesting people. . . . and holding her coat closed
across her throat she will back away,
still nodding, you call to her, to pay
for her pamphlet, trotting down the drive, wish her

the very best of luck. By the river of churning traffic,
a man in shirtsleeves, you will surprise
yourself: so this is loneliness
here. So clean. So democratic.

*

I do not mean to discourage you,
old friend: may be
you know this already, or know you will,

living a year or two here in translation;
as if your body, too,
were an odd translation.

I remember my father,
how he sat me upright on the carved lip of the bathroom tub
and cleaned my shoes, and oiled my burry hair, Sundays

before church and other random public days: awkward,
almost delicately, brushing a part in my hair
as if to make one thing perfect.

*

Rolling up his sleeves, how could he not be
disappointed, seeing what he wanted

would be as perfect as he could make it
for a moment and would change?

*

I was twelve years old, and truant,
and I paid
solemnly my quarter, the carnie barker
sniggered his promises, the vast

damp breath of the canvas tent
boomed and whispered and boomed
and I hurried in. I tried to believe
she smiled only at me,

the public woman
shining like milk, her belly
in the half-dark; amazed
how still she stood against

the placard landscape,
how deftly his wrists
flicked blue knives at her body,
outlining her body with harm:

amazed how she smiled and
stepped loose and
left her empty body
spelled on the canvas-ticking.

*

roadmaps; taxes; choices in the A-&-P; public family
     holidays;
legends (like: how Ben Franklin the realtor proposed
the nesting turkey for our national bird);

how we frame in quotation-marks
exactly what we mean
and "hesitate" to say:

Everyone can rise. Some do.
Everyone can vote. Majority rules.
The way to contain faction is to allow it.

The law describes natural process. Law is a social proscription.
I live in an orchard. I work in town.
He "celebrates" himself. You "shall assume" it.

*

Whatever city you choose some nights
you will leave the window open in heat and the voices
leak in with the sirens, the blue publicity of television,
the traffic mulling a dry wind.

You could go for an ice-cream

*

or a drive in the evening-streets.
The stores stay open fabulously late,
the mall on the rim of town a cool blue village.

And so, as if they were at home
elsewhere, we go there, late,
after supper, to visit
things. There a consoling music

seeps through the palm-trees
in their continuous daylight, the comfortable
regulated air. Our products have
proper names, which outlive us.

*

In this postcard of Boston,
geometry and vista
in the red brick
pistons on the river.

The Enlightenment ignited this machine,
its internal combustion, churning its inner
and outer clouds: Americans confuse
eloquent work devoutly with manual prayer.

Partly what you cannot see is the city
asleep, in the filmy weekday night
above the warehouses and the regular streets
of wrath and wages and offices

where futures are "speculation":
and where the city dreams
it sees, in public compensation,
the old movies that play all night.

How can you learn what they mean, those icons?
As if we had never had to learn
their fundamental grammar,
they happen out of time all night:

Harold Lloyd is hanging off a clock-face;
Marilyn Monroe laughs in her gusty skirt; Kansas is gray
and Oz is technicolor-green; a man walks into the perfect
Western sunfall and nobody smiles

like Judy Garland in *A Star is Born* and therefore
any moment in America somewhere James Mason is
        walking
into the lunging irregular sea,
in despair and out of work.

                    *

Forgive me, that I was unclear.
I did not mean "Western" as in "the West,"
but what you call *koybois filmi*:
those pastoral stories we love, too,
that are all about heroism, pride of place, grazing sheep
and real-estate. How intimately strangers
restore the civil order because they are generous
and violent, and strangers.
                    Don't worry
that your teacher drills at British English.
The language is Viking, with French gloss: trust
the flow of the syntax to keep you afloat.
Learn your prepositions; practice short-takes, hand-
        shakes, grins,
"hi" and "okay!" and "so long."

                    *

Today I wanted to show you
how the swimmers sprawled on the clean-broken shale
at Eakins Pond, beautiful as accidents
across an essential thing. One boy stood
akimbo at the apex of the stonework pier,
where the green water slowed and opened, then dove
blond into the August light. I thought of you
as he stretched in the air, and turned,
and slid through the skin of the pond. The wide blue
     rocks
were wide, and blue, and rocky qualities
only, around him in the water as he moved,
and he was what mattered.

It saddened me a little, all this need
to describe. Such a big country, so silent,
so wide and so long.
                    It's not that the truth
pre-exists you here, gathered like water
you dive into. If I deconstruct the obvious,
it's only that the American mind becomes its own
place, know-how and solitude and motion,
its sense of only-passing-through: but not the less
needy, for all that. Like a sentence already
in motion and circling, an object seeking its verb
and so—through it—a subject: like a desire, seeking
permission to desire. *The oldest country,*
Gertrude Stein says, because we have lived longer
in the twentieth century than anybody else.

I wanted to explain about the violence, inseparable
from loneliness. And from that permanent
transience: what made our uncles write
"Kilroy" on Europe and wear loud ties,
makes mothers in the city decorate the kitchen
with farm-tools, and dads in the suburb mow
and mow their lawns,

and grandmothers take evening classes
in Creative Writing, and Pottery, and Psych,
and ride the subway home, the windows sprayed with neon
runes that ache *self self* from kids afraid
they have no selves, our violence is that innocent.

So let your English teacher practice Shakespeare,
what the hell. It will serve. Read *Hamlet*—
as Zhivago did, a private man forced to perform
until he chose his role: performer. Yesterday a friend
explained the English Shakespeare knew
is spoken nowadays only in Queens.*
It's a story of accidents, survivals:
about famine and the Irish leaving home
taking with them only language and a myth
of origins: about the lonely
self-sufficient pride of immigrants,
what they make of themselves and what is made.

*

Queens is an older borough of New York.
Look at the map, far to the right:
on the edge of the country, under the green granite
breast of New England, you stop north
off the coast of New York and turn away in.

Tovarisch: do you remember the afternoon
we watched the peasant woman
wind her fat baby with the linen strips?

and how when the swaddling closed him
he stopped laughing—not
to cry but to look back?

I thought, how—I don't know how else to say it—
how Russian he looked, *pokorni'y*, resigned
after pleasure. All that day I meant to show you

the plains near Novgorod, how they spread
so like the American plains, and how odd,
lacking fences: how unenclosed.

*

The story you told in the censored letter: what
couldn't you say? Princess Betsy the cousin in Petersburg,
down on her luck, taking black bread with lard
and cups of hot water

in the marble salon. How you embroidered her
desperation, blunt pride, shame in the Romanoff
cheekbones, *Krashni'ya*-Red! And how when the Meissenware
was auctioned off,

and the Louis Quinze gone, and the statuary, she declared
une soireé toute simple in the empty ballroom, and chose
the handsomest serf-girl in the village, dressed her and
      brought her to town
in a block of ice to decorate the bare foyer.

*

What couldn't you say? I couldn't sleep,
puzzling the code—or was it metaphor?—worrying
it is your only connection:
when metaphor is more than one

idea, gathered, and you mean
to tell me I think one
idea that gathers more into itself.
When you talk that way,

is metaphor a form of desire?
It binds, like a theory of America.
But like any theory
it divides.

Is your desire—is metaphor—a form of fear?
(Desire is also fear.) America
is metaphor. Old friend forgive me,
that I can't hear your story

except to know the fact of your need
without the code to explain it; that is one
price of what we call freedom, our abashed bluntness.
Are you in danger? Can you say?

*

Since you ask, Yevgenievich, I do not forget
Leningrad—*the city impacted in ice*—the women
who stood
hours on solemn line to buy lemons,
two apiece, Georgian lemons, that smelled of soap
and singed the tongue, they were so sour; nor the lye wind

etching them in fine against the city;

nor the pyramid of
coppery lemons
they watched
diminish,
two apiece, from the straw crate,
so many green Southern moons;

nor the soldier who took six;

nor the untranslatable
fact of their waiting, shoulder
to shoulder, megalithic
in their woollen coats, their bodies
steaming in the first light.
Impossibly, they took no notice.

—this among tyrants and poets,
paired terribly.

*

Why winter here? On a high clear cold white
and blue day like this,
I went for a walk
on the State Forest Road, thinking of you

and of Trotsky,
that elegant man
of *Novi'y Mir*, who died
south of here, an ice-ax in his neck.

It stormed last night, a rage
of white quiet. Today
the woods hang tractless,
stiffened with cold,

and the snow "sublimes":
changes from crystal to gas
straightaway, without melting.
I love that in English, "sublimes":

water is water but changes
because of its cold, like a soul
passing freely to God
because of its loneliness. Where you are

the cold must be awesome.
Did he believe it could happen here,
his fluent revolution?
Or was his longing a bad map,

changing forms as his desire reformed them?
Inside the Smolny, radiating
the old betrayals,
the peasant from the Ukraine

lemon groves applauded
with one arm and the glacier marched,
freezing the feeder lake outward
from Leningrad, the starved,

and did not stop:
freezing Bukharin, and Krupskaya, and Trotsky,
freezing Mandelstam, Akhmatova, Budapest,
        Prague. . . .
I was remembering that snowy morning

in the Moscow zoo, all the strange lives
gathered in one life, and you at the empty cage
apologizing: *Ve haff at von time white Behemott,
but da Revoluzhun komms. Minny pipples eat him.*

*

I was thinking how young we were: and the *Oneigin*
     we saw,
how beautifully symmetrical it was,
country-hope and city-knowledge,
and how untrue:

Act One her longing, Act Two his.
—as if longing were finite, and human,
and only ours. We walked the snowcrust
through Decembrist Square, wanting

forgiveness, and Act Three: Tatiana remembering,
composing another letter, a map
of her clarified desire,
a longing so precisely hers

it enlarges: not for the man—Oneigin or another—
but for the form she'd imagined,
a form of belonging, truer than a man!
How young we were!

                         *

I was seven when we burned the Rosenbergs,
that simmering June. In the kitchen
my father watched his hands. My uncle
lifted me onto the table

and held me to his beard.
We are not sure our land is under us.
Today on the State Forest Road
the huge combustive snow-trucks were milling

loud where they meet
and leaving in a diesel haze
east (toward the sea) across the broad county road,
spilling salt like crazy.

                         *

By the time you get this card I will be home
from New Orleans—here it appears on the other side—, a
    trip
so hurried I don't yet know where I've been. I saw a town
with no cellars, on land as flexible as water: I saw a man
    play trumpet
in a funeral cortege and strut through a city
inside the city, graves above ground,
because set into retentive swampland,

the dead will not stay still. I saw their villas, garden
neighborhoods, their red persuasive flowers:
I thought how in Russian *krashni'ya*
means first *red*, and thus *a candle for the Mother's icon*;
and so *beautiful*, and *a girl's blush*,
and so *our first desire*—and *home*—and *us*—and therefore

eventually *Reds*. I saw the tomb of General Beauregard,
who won at Bull Run accidentally
with his starving army: so ragged
in homespun greys they stripped dead enemy boys
and wore their blues, in fog, and fought: till the Northern
    gunners
refused to fire, taking them for countrymen.

*

I wish you heartfelt "Season's Greetings," as we are both
    obliged
to call them. The gift, if it arrives, is for Stepochka's
"New Year's Tree": a bilingual Oz book (a Moscow press;
no mention of Frank Baum) by someone called "A. Volk."

(Is he for real, a Russian named "Wolf" who offers
The Wizard of Oz as *Volshebnik Isumrudnovo Goroda,
The Magician from the Fabulous Kingdom of Is*?) Is?
Both of us send love from here in Nova Zembla.

*

In this letter, Andrushka, I enclose
the roadmap you asked for. I have tried
to find you something typical:
the legend is clear, on the right.

Those pastel distinctions are the "States";
that varicose parental claw's
the Mississippi River you inquired about.
West of there, notice, most all of the States

have corners. If you stare
at them long enough they will seem
to be cracking apart,
pulling to cluster along different seams.

In most any of the spots you see here
you can ask a man
for a light. He will smile.
For some time after the message

is clear he will shake
his head and continue
to slap his body lightly,
as if putting out small fires.

*

Look at the map, the "Body Politic":
if you watch the Bering landbridge you will see the first
    Indians
were Russian, wandering east from left to right

so urgently, they became the West.
Our plane left Leningrad for Washington, then Boston
(postulated cities, cross-hatched over swamps).

Every airport looks alike; we could have found the way.
All the same, you drove us there, carried in the bags.
Susan and Vera Davidnova hugged

and promised what could be said.
We smiled too much and shook hands loud
and withholdingly, you and I, like American men

—partly, I supposed, to make you feel like one
(and only now, remembering, I see the form of it):
partly to make you look like one, an American

man—civic, withholding, affable—in that half-
exiled public place,
the trip was that risky.

*

"America," we say, after Amerigo
Vespucci, who drew the map by blind hand,
the body of his restless desire.

*

The danger of speaking desire is, a thing becomes
metaphor—and only that, its power
twice displaced, since a language is itself
the map of an original place.
I wish I could tell you America is a perfect
form of itself: city on a hill, a road

beyond history. Last night we shot pool in a road-
side bar; I thought of you. The green felt field became
semiotic, the 8-ball a made-in-America perfect
taboo: black, untouchable, a disenfranchised power
in the center of the city of the rack, a place
of prominent unimportance, feeling the self-

as-poison. The "cue"—the white ball—by itself
does not fall, but sends the others on their road
to the pocket with a secret communicative spin in place,
which in American becomes
"Body English." The danger of the power
of metaphor like this is its imperfect

balance: with it a thing is a perfect
supplement, without it a thing seems less than itself.
Remember Oz?—also a myth that has lost its power
of origins: America, 1900, controversy, and the Road
West. The Gold Standard Act was about to become
law, replacing bullion with green paper notes, trust
    placed

in promissory trust. A twister hit Kansas, lifted and
    displaced
Dorothy in her house. She landed on the witch, a perfect
hit (death by real-estate inflation). So Dorothy became
a hero to the Munchkins in the East (a joke in itself:
savage monkeys rule the West). The Yellow Brick Road
led to the center—"Oz." as in "ounces"—an emerald
    power

where citizens in tinted spectacles banked on the power
of promises: alternate Kansas, the happy other-place.
Dorothy with the Lion, Scarecrow, and Tinman took to
    the road
(she with her animal, vegetable, and mineral friends: a
    perfect
union). They broke the green illusion, met the wizard,
    himself
a loveable Barnum humbug. Still he helped them to
    hope, to become

their talents, and go home. So Judy Garland sings the
    perfect place
lies "Over the Rainbow": figuration's power to become
a new self, as the country lies: down the promising
    golden road.

*

I can tell you
what I would like
to be able to tell you:

a country where men touch,
connected by
a simple mutuality.

—though we do not know clearly what we want
when we want that,
camerado, Comrade.

—here where the swollen light
gathers above the sidewalks
of my ordinary town

and the loud voluptuous cars appear,
circling slowly, and pause,
and lurch past, purring and fuming.

I can tell you
summer nights took the color of nickels
weaving the blue streets

in somebody's father's DeSoto
and we pushed laughing
and watched the tanned hopeful girls

with clear hair, their Pawnee gentlenesses,
behind the windows
of somebody's father's Chevrolet

in the closed air
and the simmering public music
moving their mouths as if singing

whose names we did not remember
and thrashed against them earnestly
across the plush leatherette, pushing

into scared girls, the cryptic
rivers of their bodies, finding there
all we had thought to ask for.

*

It will happen to you,
standing in a clearing:
suddenly two

curling roads converge
their dusts, odd short buildings
rise and the sidewalk hardens, neighbors

gossip and vote, the war is over
and the boys come home
without polio, the Fourth of July

walks on its stilts
of light, the football team
parades among chrysanthemums, amazingly

the ornamental girls still shimmer their pompoms,
the sad-eyed butcher with feathers in his hair recognizes you,
and you cannot remember when you did not pay rent.

It is an ordeal
by innocence, standing on Main Street.
Over the bandshell the glass clouds hurry.

How loyal
the ordinary air, bending around you.
You choose the air.

You walk through your choices, knowing
to walk is to fall
short, falling

with stupid confidence.
They have always been strangers.
Implausibly, you live here.

*

At last, you write, your visa has come through.
You're moving to California,
and I will seldom see you.
California. I worry

for your quiet wife, for her family
impossibly behind you. Maybe one summer
I could drive the six days
to visit you all. Stepán

Andreievich will be naturalized.
You will be tanned,
welcoming me. We will sit
at the marina, you and I,

with our feet on the brass rail
and marvel at ourselves. We will be
older. I will still admire your courage
of illusion;

you will laugh that I worried,
and know why. We will be older.
Maybe it will all seem natural,
the past like a fat sealed letter.

Maybe in the next act, years later,
Tatiana loves Oneigin again,
the man, in retrospection,
walking under grey-green birches

and a squirrel chittering.
May be. Let me know,
Andrei Yevgenievich.
You have the address.

IV

El Zoologico

We had to hurry
to catch the open silver train
that jingled the rim of the park. It was Sunday,
early, summer-hazy, and we imagined
we were the only travellers awake

in the public gardens. —only also the quick
Catalonian boys, who jumped from the red hibiscus
hedge and ran along the track, grabbed
expertly at the caboose
railing and spilled aboard,

laughing. So we began, together, by continuing:
past alphabetical bivalves and corals,
the musk of the snake installation,
past the bypass to the marsupial pavilion,
the fish.

At each stop our driver pronounced
the names of the animals carefully,
an invitation, with a rinse of soft dialect:
*guella del paradiso, cigne
cantor.* In a cork tree the ibex

wondered; *flamencos* on their saffron legs
displayed themselves; among bamboo
the pale *cigüeña* wattled its nest,
that brings luck to the village it chooses.

Under the lucid foreign signs:
the moose in her paddock with her Cleopatra eyelids,
the muledeer swivelling her ears (toward what?),
the black goat peeling a sapling:
all doubly strange,

locked in their permanent mornings.
Then the train hurried on a little
faster and we could not account for all that happened:
la pantera full of sliding vowels,
the jackal that chewed and stammered and stared;

prohibito (the guide warned) *tocar los animales,*
no molestar; in the distance we passed
something whiskered and whorling,
like the noiseless intelligent horses
painted floating on cave-walls;

and the small dark man
who terrified his daughter
at the porpoise-lagoon, swinging her over the rim,
¡*hola*! ¡*mira*!, rolling his cruel r's,
while she made little mewling noises and held on.

Then suddenly monkeys! some who looked intelligent;
who picked their fleas, who chittered and panted, who ate shit;
some exhibiting behavior on their hemisphere of rock;
cinnamon monkeys, and sawdust, and talc,
and odd pastels; monkeys the flavors of smoke;

dozens of species-grammars, *los monos*! families
and clans and colonies, and braided unlikely alliances. . . .
I wanted to hang around a little longer, beside
the anthropoid madonna with her stroking tail,
but we could not stop:

not till the unique white
Gorilho de Barcelona, in his glass box,
that we had come so far for.
Filthy, lice-laced, untranslatable,
he rolled his churning shoulders,

mindful of us, and turned away. The train
paused; we disembarked; he seemed impossible.
I wonder how long we stood there, without speaking,
breathing his thick afflicted smell—?
It seemed ages,

watching him grunt and look back, watching
him hide his hands between his knees (he watched us
    watching)
and bellow once, and stop—just like that—and lean to
    himself,
and work an itch, scraping a horny finger at his chest
as if he might find—what was it

we wanted?—something or other, something
remarkable, something
lacking, from that vast and abstract body.

In the darkness of the body

you come to a field
of white and yellow manzanilla flowers
spread along a hillside
soft in its lines as chalk.

You wade through the huge color.
As if they were picked
and floated over water, they ride
easily their strong stalks, cloud-heavy,
heavy with camomile.

Sometimes they swim in waves, giving way
to a wind as if a vast slow hand
brushed across them. Then their pollen
shakes loose and silts
across the blond petals and stains the ground

and stains the hand
a deep specific yellow. You may catch a few grains,
fine and geometric as a salt,
and dark, and deeply plushed.
How lightly they sit across your fingertips!

They carry the smell of the field
steeping in the wide light. Can you
taste it? Taste
that one: the gold flake on your thumbnail.
You bend to it, hovering your lips.

You hold your breath
a little, out of fear
you will lose it,
it is so exact.
It is so exact! A little bitterness

resolves across the tongue. So the body is
invented, its bright particularity
earned, grain by grain. You taste
the field, and the taste of yourself
adjusts itself a little.

Narcissus

Narcissus is sad on the water.
Though he is very beautiful,
carved of clarified light and floating
back to him like a fine boat,
he is dissatisfied

and cannot find the singing.
He is exactly sad
because he is in love
with that face, the image
of the self's intrigues, and because

to love is to lose the self
and so he loses what he loves, exactly
as he loves it, pain for pain
paid out on the green and
changing water:

and the slow sad waste of pain
and the losses
and the change that is a kind of wind
wrinkling the water
are a horror to him.

It is not the story of Echo and her bell
that is the sad story. She is a sky
passing over water, succulent and singular and blue,
without horizons. Her loss is
completely herself skimming toward him, asking

how shall I find you finding
herself *find you find you*.
Though she is without a body she is not sad,
it is no matter. Maybe
she arrives, or doesn't; they will not touch.

Or maybe her singing is a kind of body,
carnal of the blue sky, leaving
substantive footprints.
Maybe. But
it is a hard thing to say, living

as a man does in the body:
to learn to love loss
as the deep law,
love and relinquish.
And love. And relinquish.

When the water broke,

my mare stretched longer.
She breathed fast steam.
Where her bulk settled the shape of her
in snow melted and formed again,
puckered in iceballs: she could not see
where she worked
her body heavily.

I could have run through my fear as through an old
        house,
the wooden hall, across the long veranda,
and run toward the moon aligned on the fence post.
And I thought, if it is wild,
that vast space, its violence must be
formal as an animal.
I hid among planets. Snow hung
in the anesthetic air.

And when the cold began
to dive, folding its face against
those long legs—pastern muzzle ears—
when it slid
and entered, its first heat
slizzling through air—
spine belly haunch—all body
in its sheeting of white veins

no other space seemed possible
than this space,
specific in mystery.
Which was the background here?
and which the figure? The mare
watched me sidelong as I lifted it,
tethered and steaming,
to peel the sac:

                    the littlehorse
shook itself loose from its flesh material
and lifted itself—the idea of it!—and stood a moment
between its mother's legs,
the leg of them
breathing and
disjunct,
before she spoke, throating
low once, and rose to it, and turned to nurse.

I Write

and it is your name.
As if in outline, curled, the letters of your name
lie perfectly, their curves an empty body
filling with a plain slow water.

So, strange, in time, this new thing
swells in its form like a second fashioning.
It is not my idea of you, not
exactly, but it watches me
with your clear green eyes. It is rounded

and shaded, like your body's hollows
I could not, myself, have adequately told.
Like you it shakes your narrow shoulders
when you have slept a long time on your left side,
turned from me. So perhaps I am only a little jealous, now,

of this new thing between us: because it is
also your body, and foreign to me
as it fills slowly with itself, stretches
over the white sheet and rises,
shivers to dress in the New Year's cold

and makes as if to go,
entering the world beyond this one.
We don't talk much—
or rather, I do all the talking.
In the hallway on an empty page

you scribble a little, maybe
a wrong number but a gesture, almost
tender; recalling you, I watch it
lope out, coltish and awkwardly formal
at the end: into the exacting morning light,

down the numbered avenue and the frost and salt and
     thickening snow,
turning up the collar of your cotton jacket,
digging your long hands deep in the pockets,
down along the sidewalk among slender women
in snoods and overcoats, among strangers with pale lips.

"Landscape with Mares and Foals"

In that field
is open summer.
    Under a copper beech
three mares graze
    almost without motion, and the small wind

turning the leaves through dimensions of gold light
    does not lift their manes.
One chestnut-roan,
    the sorrel half in shadow,
the white in sun who snuffs at a pink-flowered weed,

    arching down her neck:
they stand
    across the green turf
grazing the light carefully
    tangled in the low grasses.

And so they are three times silent,
    the mares:
in innocent flesh, in color-and-poise,
    in composition:
how George Stubbs has gathered them

    as in a Grecian frieze,
the planes of their bodies
    aligned as in procession
toward the older gods.
    Only the two colts

swagger a little, pushing
    to nurse, and flap their ears,
and turn their flanks at angles against the round
    horizon their mothers make
with their bodies against the sky,—

defining depth
and axis, suggesting a fuller time
        this moment interrupts
without sacrifice, the moment
        given freely, like milk.

It's when I'm tired
        of human longing
and think the world
        is not a foreign place
enough, but too familiar

        mirrors-of-mirroring-needs, I open my eyes
to it and return, as if I could:
        to the painted summer and the shadow pools
and the end of the dream
        of reason. I remember

how he acknowledged this calm
        through knowledge,
which was to say dissection—
        the several stinkings of the poor body,
how it comes, and moves, and leaves—

        and the illustrations,
his first work, *A Compleat New System
        of Midwifery*, six years
of laboratory and the sooted lamps,
        opening the bodies

of drowned pauper women
        to watch the children
strangled there
        who might have turned
differently

and breathed,
and knew their convolutions
    and drew them from inside,
what the body contains
    and is:

an art schooled in death
    and accuracy.
At thirty five he turned
    to horses. He must have loved them
first as form, and so he drew

    out this field of sun-feeding
clovers where the mares
    graze empowered:
as if their bodies were necessary,
    the mass of this full

and disencarnate light: not because he loved them
    but because they are—
even the sorrel filly, that way
    turned from the waist off to the left a little,
half in shade, the silent one—the one without a foal, or
    not yet.

In light

and first May the plumtree
opens, out of a central calm
astonished into blossom.

The solitude of the dark wood
emerges, pistil and stamen
and fleshy plumflower, breaking

through:
into historical air
and the luminous

common heat: if the world
did resemble the soul
at the center we would know

no other body,
walking the mown rows of the orchard
in May and the scent

of sweet-vinegar
winter-softened
brown fallen plums: for an hour,

pierced by an exact desire,
I knew the self could be
relinquished. This is the afterlife,

this body.